Blessed

A SPIRITUAL JOURNEY

EVA TRACY

Illustrated by: Madeleine Earls

WestBow Press books may be ordered through booksellers or by contacting:

WestBow Press
A Division of Thomas Nelson & Zondervan
1663 Liberty Drive
Bloomington, IN 47403
www.westbowpress.com
844-714-3454

ISBN: 979-8-3850-2895-5 (sc)
ISBN: 979-8-3850-2896-2 (e)

Library of Congress Control Number: 2024913701

Print information available on the last page.

WestBow Press rev. date: 08/27/2024

CONTENTS

DEDICATION

This book is dedicated to my parents Eva and Richard Earls. Two earth angels who taught me about God, how to love, and to be a generous spirit.

ACKNOWLEDGEMENTS

Many beautiful souls have helped in the creation of my book. I would like to thank my husband, Phil Tracy, for his incredible love and support. His intelligence and profound kindness guided me during the process of writing my book.

My very creative and free -spirited daughter, Madee Earls for her lovely paintings and her wisdom. My sons, Skyler and Dylan Tracy for their words of encouragement and enthusiasm.

My grandparents, Carl and Carrie Hellmers for nurturing me. I will never forget all of the sunny hours spent with my grandpa as we wrote stories together.

My brother and sister, Ricky Earls and Elisabeth Pearse who made our life's journey, with all of it's ups and downs, extremely enjoyable!

To my most cherished friend, Stacy Hoover, with whom I have shared countless magical adventures. Thank you for always believing in me and pushing me toward success.

To Kathy Fraidy, my sweet friend, who emboldened me to finish my book.

To Janie Dean, my dear and brilliant friend who edited my book. I can't thank you enough! I will remember fondly our afternoons spent at Starbuck's working on this project.

To George and Bernie Hellmers, my aunt and uncle, who have always been there for me. They have imbued my life with love, peace, and happiness.

Lastly, I wish to thank my team at Westbow Press. They have been amazing to work with. Especially Janine David, who has guided me through this process every step of the way with kindness and professionalism.

FOREWORD

*W*elcome to *Blessed.* This book has been a long time in the making. Every story in the book, as incredulous as some of the happenings may seem, is true. The only details that have been altered are the names of most of the people and some of the places.

My book is a means to allow you, the reader, to develop a closer relationship with God. It is not meant to exclude anyone, but to relate my life story in a way that will hopefully bring peace and joy to others. It is meant to illuminate the lives of precious people who may be dealing with depression, fear, and anxiety. In turn, I hope it will replace these feelings with knowing that you are loved beyond measure and that there is hope awaiting you. A relationship with the Divine is yours for the asking. You can find peace on earth and be a light for others.

Have an open mind and an open heart as you travel with me on this soul searching journey. May every blessing be yours.

THE JOURNEY

*W*hen I was only five years old, I had a truly extraordinary, life-changing experience. I wouldn't tell anyone exactly what happened, what I had been through until several years later. I thought it was supposed to be a secret - a secret between me and God.

On that fateful summer afternoon in 1970, I had been playing with my brother, Ricky, and sister, Elisabeth, in our backyard. We are all a year and a half apart. I am the oldest and Liz is the youngest with Ricky sandwiched in between. We had been playing catch, entertaining ourselves with card games on the patio, riding our bikes, and hopping on the stepping stones. The stepping stones were the lovely traditional pavers that were approximately twelve inches round with tiny pebbles on the surface. We were hopping from one to another while trying not to touch the grass. If you touched the grass, you had fallen into the sea of fire and were out of the game.

My mom and grandma were outside with us as well. My grandma lived right next door and was over almost every day. It was truly a blessing growing up with our grandparents living so close. I treasured the evenings when I was invited over to their home for dinner. My grandma was an amazing cook and my grandma, grandpa, and I would dine together while watching one of my grandpa's favorite shows *"Gunsmoke"*. Anyway, Mom and Grandma spent that afternoon sitting on the patio sipping iced tea and watching us play. They also joined us at our weathered picnic table on the back patio to play Old Maid and Go Fish. The picnic table was covered with markings from our crayons and still a bit sticky from the watermelon we shared from the night before. As we played Old Maid with characters on the cards such as Fifi Fluff, Greenthumb Gert, and Milkman Mo, my mom helped Elisabeth with the game. Every so often, my mom's laughter lingered on the afternoon breeze.

Later in the afternoon, the sky had grown somber and overcast. The deep, dark purple sky with its shifting clouds caused a wave of anxiety to sweep over me. I had an ominous feeling that something bad was about to happen. Shortly afterwards, while we were playing catch, Ricky fell down on one of the stepping stones and cut his knee very badly. Grandma told me to run inside and grab the hydrogen peroxide and gauze bandages. When she was younger, Grandma had wanted to be a nurse, and we relied on her knowledge and ability to care for us. I ran inside and brought back the supplies as quickly as I could. We had just finished bandaging him up when the rain started coming down. Ricky and I sat on the patio for a little while longer while everyone else had retreated inside. I hated seeing him in so much pain, but I was relieved that he was going to be okay. I thought to myself that his getting injured was connected to the ominous feeling that I had experienced earlier. His accident had taken a lot out of him and the storm had become quite nasty! The rain was coming down sideways and more of our patio was getting wet. We decided it was also time for us to go inside so I helped him hobble to his room.

My mom and grandma helped Ricky into his bed while speaking words of comfort over him, reassuring him that he was going to be fine; he just needed some rest. Elisabeth mused herself by playing with the myriad of toys in his room. From his window, I could see flashes of lightening and hear the rumbling of thunder outside. His room was very small, and I, not wanting to be in the way, stood leaning with my right shoulder against the door frame that was directly across from the window. I was holding my Raggedy Ann in my left hand while watching them tuck him into bed. Raggedy Ann was the doll that I chose more often than not to sleep with at night. She smelled of perfume and her cheeks were a bit too rosy: a condition of my playing with my mom's makeup.

Just then lightning came in through the window above Ricky's bed and struck me in the abdomen. My mom recalls that it all happened so quickly. She said that that lightning came in through the window, hit me, and I hit the floor. I remember it differently. I don't recollect any pain, but I knew that I had been hit. In my five- year old mind, the bolt looked like an electric finger. The electric finger was meant just for me like it was pointing me out. It felt like I had been jabbed in the stomach. I was in a state of shock as I looked down at my stomach. When I looked back up toward my family, everyone sounded muffled and time seemed to pass in slow motion. It was as though I was in a vacuum or cocoon. My body started to fall backwards. The last thing that I remember was the expression of horror on my mom's face. I was dead before I even hit the floor.

I think that it is important to mention that the glass above my brother's bed didn't shatter, nor was my stomach burned or marred in any matter. My whole life I have believed that I was struck by actual, physical lightning. However, after delving deeper, was it a supernatural occurrence? Was it something that the devil meant to harm me that God turned into something amazing? Or was the bolt sent by God to show me that heaven and hell certainly exist? I won't have the answer to these questions until I am standing before God in my heavenly home. Much later in life, I would see the divine, Jesus and the Holy Spirit, pass through walls. And on one terrifying incident, I saw a demonic creature looking like a man clothed in silver from head to toe, run through a sliding glass door without breaking the glass. Whether the lightning bolt was an element of the physical world or the supernatural, it sent me on a wild journey.

The next series of events, are without a doubt, the most horrific occurrences that have ever happened to me. I was still wearing the same clothes that I had on earlier that day and my long blonde hair was still in braids, but I was now flat on my back with my arms and legs stretched out, and I was falling at an incredible speed. I was in a pit and when I looked over my shoulder, it looked bottomless. Not only was I falling, I was also spinning around and around. It was like being on a terrible carnival ride that you can't get off of. There was an eerie, green light coming from below and there appeared to be a substance resembling smoke billowing upwards. I was overwrought - totally panic-stricken! I was extremely aware of my stomach churning. The pit was of a muddy color and in its crevices, sat little demons. Some of the demons were crawling along the face of the pit. They were very short, reddish-brown creatures with rat like tails, and large, pointed ears. Some of them held their hands close to their faces laughing at me as I continued to fall and spin. They terrified me and I was filled with a feeling of hopelessness. I had absolutely no control over my body; the only thing that I could move was my head.

I would have done just about anything to remove myself from the perilous situation that I found myself in. I wondered, "Who can help me?" I knew that my mother couldn't, and my only chance would be a higher power: God. I called out to Him in a weak, little voice. I thought that if the little demons heard me calling out to God that they would laugh at me even more. After I called out, "Dear God, please help me," nothing changed. I continued my unrelenting decent. I began to think, "I don't care who hears me or what they think about me. I want out!!" It was very difficult to catch my breath, but with everything that I had left, I screamed as loud as I could, "Dear God, please help me!!"

He did.

I was transported from that horrible pit where there was no hope, only despair, to the edge of heaven. I have no idea how I was transferred. It has been blocked from my memory-something that is meant to remain mysterious to me. My clothes that I had on earlier were gone and in their place, was a long, white robe. My hair was loose and flowing behind me. There was nothing nor anyone around me except for amazing blue skies and great, pure white, puffy clouds in a vast expanse that went on and on as far as the eye could see. Even though I was the only soul around, I was not afraid. I was completely content. I felt as though my entire being was beaming with joy. Most of all, I was thankful for being rescued!! I tried to walk, and that process was very difficult and comedic. The large, cotton candy shaped clouds came all the way up to my knees. I thought the only way to walk would be to pick my leg up and try to step over them. I remember laughing at myself while bending over glancing at the clouds beneath my feet, realizing I could walk right through them.

A second later when I looked up, where there had been nothing except for blue skies and clouds, there was now a tunnel with a great light coming from inside it. The outside wall of the tunnel had light shining through it, and I could see every color of the rainbow prismed in it. The colors were so rich and vibrant. In front of the tunnel stood a man. His dark brown hair fell just above His shoulders and His skin tone was of a lovely olive color. His eyes were crystal blue and His bright smile made me feel like I was home. I had been brought up in church and bible school and He didn't look exactly like the pictures that I had seen of Him. He was still easily recognizable. There wasn't a shadow of doubt in my mind. It was Jesus. I was so excited to see him!

We spoke to one another without actually talking aloud. I don't remember opening my mouth to speak. It was more like a mental tennis match where we bounced our thoughts to one another. With His right hand raised, He welcomed me with a warm, "Hello." I replied, "Hey, it's You!" My voice was filled with excitement. He then told me that I had to go back, that it wasn't my time yet. I said, "No, I don't want to go back". It was not that I didn't want to return to my wonderful childhood. I didn't want to leave Heaven. In the short time that I was there, on the outskirts of heaven, I felt such a profound sense of peace that I have never felt before or since.

The reason that I believe this was the outskirts of heaven is because I didn't see anyone else. I have heard accounts from other people who have died, gone to heaven, and then returned to earth. Many of them say that they were greeted by loved ones who had passed on. The only one I saw was Jesus, and our encounter was awesome.

Jesus said, "You have to go back. There are things that you are supposed to do that no one can do but you." Still, I continued to beseech the Lord. "No, I like it here." He looked down, sighed, and shook His head. He came over to the edge of the cloud where I was standing and said, "Look down. Your family is crying out for you." He turned me around and where there were once endless skies, I could now see hundreds of tiny houses, but the roofs were off. I could see people moving about in their homes, going about their daily business. It was pretty fascinating! Then, He helped me to focus on my house. My family had moved my body from where it had fallen and placed me between the dining room table and the refrigerator. My grandma was on her knees and had my head in her lap. It was so strange watching them from above as they tried to help me. My brother was standing over my left shoulder as my sister crouched near my feet. My mom was sobbing overcome with grief as she held onto the open freezer door for support, she had been passing ice to my grandmother. She was sobbing so hard that her knees kept buckling underneath her. My grandma was trying to put ice down my throat in an effort to revive me. She looked up to heaven screaming for God to help. My body had already begun to turn blue. I was moved with compassion and told Jesus that I would go back. He was happy with this decision. Then, I panicked, "I don't know how to get back." He said, "All you have to do is jump. Your soul will find its way back to your body because there is a silver thread that connects them." I took a leap of faith and jumped. I don't remember traveling from heaven to earth; I can only imagine what that might have been like. Did I soar gracefully through the air or did I plummet clumsily looking like Alice as she fell into the white rabbit's hole? It is a mystery. When my soul made its way back, it entered my body head first and then had to straighten out. It was quite a shock! My eyes blinked open. With tears still streaming down my mom's face, my family gently helped me to my feet as they hugged me. They were very relieved and thankful that I was okay.

My mom took me to the hospital, and they performed a considerable amount of tests on me. They brought me into a room, where the nurses put long rods on my head. The doctor was standing behind a glass with the control panel. They told me to lie down on the table and pretend like I was sleeping. They were testing me for any brain damage that I may have incurred during the incident. I couldn't keep still. After laying there for a few moments, I popped up and said, "I'm okay. I'm ready to go home." Of course, this prolonged the testing because they would have to start over. After what seemed like an eternity, they let me choose a toy and released me. I couldn't wait for Dad to get home from work so that I could tell him how I was struck by lightning, went to the hospital, and got a new stuffed toy. At this time, I thought that I wasn't supposed to share that I met Jesus. Looking back, I'm really not sure what led me to that conclusion. I honestly wish that I would have shared every detail with my parents immediately. I know they would have been enthralled and more importantly they would have believed me.

This forever life changing experience had lasted for just a few moments. Amazingly, in that brief time, I saw part of hell, the outskirts of heaven, and met my Savior face to face. Due to this journey, I have never doubted that there is a God and that Jesus is as much alive today as He was two thousand years ago.

This experience opened a spiritual door. I didn't see Jesus again until I was eleven years old. By then I had grown into a chubby, nerdy girl with oily, dark blonde hair and quite a bit of acne. I had very little self-confidence. I was very different from the bright, petite, five-year old that was filled with moxie. Some of the reasons for the change included the passing of my father and starting a new school. I had to form new friendships and had gained a lot of weight. One night, while I was sleeping, Jesus and Mary came to me in a dream. Mary said, "Go tell them that my son is alive." Jesus agreeing said, "Tell them that I'm alive." Since I had very little self-confidence, I wondered how I would handle this task. I don't remember exactly what I said, but there was definitely hesitation on my part. They urged me to let people know that Jesus is still alive, so I reluctantly agreed. I worried over how I would tell others and wondered if they would even listen to an eleven-year old girl.

The next morning when I got up, I pondered how I would carry out this enormous task. I feared that people wouldn't believe me and that I would be made fun of. During one of my classes that day, I thought, "This is it. I'm just going to raise my hand, stand up and say 'Jesus is alive', and then quickly sit back down." As I was about to stand, I became very nervous and my hands became cold and clammy. I was afraid that my classmates might think that I was a bit crazy. Then the brilliant idea came to me that maybe I should tell my family first and see how they would respond.

That afternoon when I got home from school, I shared with my mom and Elisabeth that when I was struck by lightning when I was five years old, I met Jesus. This did not go over well. They started laughing so hard that my mom had tears running down her face, and Elisabeth was doubled over with laughter saying, "Get her Mom, she thinks she saw Jesus." I insisted, but they couldn't hear over the gales of laughter. I thought to myself that it was probably a good idea that I didn't share this information with my class considering that my own family found it so amusing. Even though I felt terribly guilty for letting Mary and Jesus down, I thought that for the time being, I should continue to keep this information to myself. This is exactly what I have done -until I was saved.

I have since shared my story with family and friends. When you read it, you have a choice to make. You might think that I am crazy or that I hallucinated the whole thing, but I know that my experience was real. Jesus is alive and well! Your destiny is in your hands. You have the power to spend eternity with Him in Heaven. One of my pastors once said that people spend more time planning their vacations than planning for eternity, and I believe this to be true. The Bible states that if you call upon the name of the Lord, you will be saved. We cannot earn a place in heaven; it is a gift from God for those who believe in Him. I have the peace and reassurance of knowing that when I leave this world, I will be instantaneously in heaven with God. I've seen it. It is my prayer that you will join me there in paradise. Until then, I will long to see what lies beyond the other side of the tunnel.

The Journey Scripture

Trust in the Lord with all your heart;
And lean not unto your own understanding.
In all thy ways acknowledge Him,
And He shall direct your paths.

Proverbs 3:5-6

Prayer Notes

BLESSED

A few years had passed by since my extraordinary encounter with Jesus and our lives changed drastically. My father, who I loved and adored, passed away when I was seven years old. He had suffered for many years from stomach cancer and succumbed to this horrible disease at the age of forty-seven. Dad was one of the kindest people that I have ever known. He filled our lives with love, music, and adventures. An example of his love and thoughtfulness is when I was around five or six years old and had contracted pneumonia. I had seen advertisements on the T.V. for weeks that the *Wizard of Oz* would be shown soon. The movie looked awesome, and I couldn't wait to see it. I waited with great anticipation! Every day, I would ask mom and dad, "Is today the day we get to watch the *Wizard of Oz*?" When the day finally arrived, I was so sick that I thought I would miss it. I had spent several days in bed, and I was very weak. Our family doctor even made a house call to check on me. My dad, knowing how desperate I was to watch it, picked me up and carried me to the dining room, where our T.V. sat in the corner so that we could watch during supper. He had a chair all set up for me right in front of the T.V. with cushions and a cozy blanket. I was enthralled! I watched for about an hour when I surrendered to fatigue. It was with a heavy heart that I pulled myself away and crawled back into bed. My parents promised me that it would play again in the future and filled me in the next morning with everything that I had missed.

Another time, we were having a party at our home and my dad had been barbecuing in our back yard. There were about thirty guests, but I don't remember the occasion. My brother, Ricky, and I were in the back yard with dad when he put a white chef's hat on my head and said that I could help with the coals. The party was nearing its end, and it was time to start cleaning up. My job was to take the coals, that were still pretty hot, with a pair of tongs and place them in a bucket. It was fun, and I was doing a decent job when I dropped one of the coals on the ground. I was having a problem picking it up off the ground using the tongs so I decided I'll just use my hand: bad decision. The coals were still very hot. I started screaming! My dad who had stepped right inside our back door came running to my side. He said that my mom was going to kill him. He came up with the idea for us to sneak back inside the house, and we would then crawl our way to the front bathroom where we kept the medicine in the linen closet. We crawled through and beside our guests' legs and made our way to the dining room table that we hid underneath for a few moments. Quite a few of our guests found this to be highly entertaining.

Mom was in the adjacent room, the kitchen, and there was fear of getting found out. We crawled through my sister's and my bedroom and finally made it to the bathroom. By the time we got there, we were both giggling. My hand still hurt, but dad had taken my mind off of it with his game of not wanting mom to find out. He put medicine on my wound and bandaged me up as mom was knocking on the door questioning what was going on. We continued to giggle as dad replied, "Oh we are fine. We will be out in a moment." I am sure that mom had a long chat with dad after the party.

After dad passed, mom raised the three of us with the help of my grandparents, who lived right next door. Mom juggled three jobs just to make ends meet. I know that she was absolutely exhausted most of the time, but for us, she always tried to have a smile on her face. She had a bubbly personality and did the best she could to make us feel loved and secure.

Mom had a gorgeous singing voice. When she was in college, she had studied singing and Opera. When we were little, due to her love for music, on Sundays she sang at a few churches. One evening, she was walking up to one of the churches for choir practice with a cake in her hands. Two teen-aged boys approached her with a gun and threatened to shoot her if she didn't hand over her purse. She refused. They grabbed onto the strap of her purse, and she held on to it while jumping back and forth from one foot to another, while balancing her cake saying, "You can't shoot me. I'm a moving target." When they went to shoot her, their gun fell apart. Thankfully, two other choir members were walking toward the church as my mom was being attacked. The teen-aged boys panicked, flipped over her cake, and darted off. My mom looked down at her cake dejectedly and said, "Oh my goodness!! You have ruined my cake! Come back here and clean this up!" The choir members consoled her and helped her into the church.

Mom was also very protective of us while we were growing up. From the time I was eleven until twenty, we would perform plays over the summer with one of the church groups, Salem United Church of Christ. When I was thirteen, I had a huge crush on William who was seventeen and already had quite the reputation for being a ladies' man. He was very attractive, charming, and reminded me of Jimmy Stewart in *It's A Wonderful Life*. On the closing afternoon of the plays, the director would throw a cast party in celebration for all of our hard work. He would either take us to Farrell's Ice Cream Parlor or have a swim party at one of the clubs. It was at one of these swim parties that William kept following me around to chat. We were standing not too far from the pool in our swimsuits, when my mom approached him. She whispered something in his ear and he ran and jumped into the pool. My mom just smiled at me and walked off. I thought this was very strange. I went over where my friends were sitting to join in their conversation. A few moments later, William came and sat by me and said, "Do you know what your mother said to me?" I replied, "No. I have no idea. What did she say?" He replied, "She told me to stay away from you and then she put a handful of ice down my swim shorts!" I started laughing. Needless-to-say, William and I never dated. However, we remained friends.

During the school year, I occupied my time doing homework, and taking voice and dance lessons. I am not sure when it happened, but somehow my family had slacked off on going to church. Sundays had evolved into the day that we slept late and then prepared for the coming week. We did chores and then helped grandma get ready for family dinner. Family dinner was a major event each week. Besides the six of us, there was extended family that would join us. Grandma would always prepare a delicious feast including dessert. Once dinner was over and the kitchen was cleaned, we would partake in games such as Pokeno and Bingo and gamble with our loose change- nothing larger than a quarter. We were collecting delightful memories that we would revisit for the rest of our lives.

One day when I was thirteen, it dawned on me that something was lacking. Our lives were so busy with tons of activity, yet I felt that something was missing. After taking a closer look, I realized that something was someone: God. I still prayed, but not like I used to, and after much thought, I concluded that my family had quit going to church.

I decided to speak to my mom about my feelings and stated that I wanted to start going to church again. She agreed that it was a good idea. At times, other family members would join me, and sometimes I went alone. I loved going with my grandpa who was one of the kindest and most intelligent people that I have ever known. He had a profound love for us that was revealed in the way that he truly took an interest in what was going on in our lives. I could talk to him about anything and he would open my eyes to a list of solutions. No matter how busy he was, he would stop what he was working on and immerse himself in our problems, no matter how large or trivial. He was the very definition of love.

When I was fourteen, I made my Confirmation in the Catholic Church. Confirmation is one of the seven sacraments, where one receives a special outpouring of the Holy Spirit. This is comparable to the Day of Pentecost when the Holy Spirit descended upon the apostles in fire and wind. I had studied very hard in my CCD classes and usually raised my hand if they needed someone to read scripture. I was painfully shy at the time and thought that reading aloud in front of the class might help me to get over my fear. It didn't cure the problem, but it certainly did help. I didn't make any lifelong friends in the class, but I was well-liked and some would ask me questions about what we were studying.

One night before Confirmation, they held a small ceremony for us. One boy and one girl from the class of about sixty were chosen to read scripture. I was thrilled and nervous that I was chosen! At the end of the evening, we met in the Sanctuary for the lighting of the candles. Each student was given a blessed candle and the lighting of these was to symbolize God's spirit alive in each of us; it was to remind us to let our light shine before men. During this part of the ceremony, I was chosen once again out of a handful of students to help light the candles. What happened next was kind of odd. Instead of receiving the light off of a neighbor's candle, many gathered around me waiting specifically for me to light their candles. I was overwhelmed with emotion. As you read this, it might not seem like such a big deal, but for me, that evening turned out to be a highlight in my amazingly awkward teenage years.

A couple of days later, we took part in our Confirmation. The ceremony was a simple and lovely affair. We just had to wait our turn sitting in the pews then walk to the altar. The priest would then anoint us and we were to say, "Amen". It sounds easy enough, but while I was walking toward the altar, I kept hearing a creaking sound coming from the front right corner of the church. By the time that I reached the altar, I was completely mesmerized. The creaking noise was God peeling part of the ceiling up and I saw the Holy Spirit descending very slowly in the form of a dove. He descended feet first with His wings outstretched. He appeared very regal. I kept looking up at Him with wonderment and joy totally ignoring the priest. By this time, the priest had repeated himself, for my benefit, about four times. Then my Aunt Hilda who was standing next to me as my sponsor, gently tapped me on my shoulder and said, "Say Amen, say Amen!" I quickly responded, "Oh yeah, Amen." My aunt was giggling and I was slightly embarrassed as we headed back to our seats. After seeing the Holy Spirit, I felt like I was glowing for days. The entire process of studying the Bible in my CCD classes and then being in the Holy Spirit's presence sparked a fire within me. There was a desire not just to say my prayers before bedtime, but to sit in quietude reflecting on God and my life, asking for God to bless those I loved, as I dwelt in stillness waiting for Him to illuminate various aspects of my life.

This was not the only time that I saw the Holy Spirit. Many years later, while I was rehearsing one evening with the choir at The Abundant Life Fellowship, I saw the Holy Spirit appear off to our right side, hovering close to the ceiling. He was in the form of a dove and enormous in size. He was about four feet long which is extremely large for a dove. It was very hard to concentrate on what we were singing as I didn't want to take my eyes off of Him. He stayed only for a few moments and then flew through one of the back walls of the church. This occurrence filled me with bliss. It is equally comforting and awe inspiring to be in the presence of the Lord.

It is so important for us to spend quality time with God as it opens our hearts and minds. We become more loving and more aware of the needs of others. When we pray and meditate, we are communicating with our Heavenly Father on a very deep and personal level.

I begin each day with a cup of coffee and my Bible and read at my dining room table before anyone else is up. I feel that during this time God prepares me for my day. I become aware of obstacles that I will need to overcome and when to keep my mouth shut! There have been days when I have needed to talk to God throughout my day for strength and direction, but also, times when I desire to send up prayers of gratitude. As of late, that has become my word: Gratitude. We have so much to be thankful for everyday! To listen to the lilting of a bird's song; to be greeted with a sunrise every morning; to glory at the magnificent brushstrokes of an afternoon sky; food on the table; loved ones to share our lives with. These are all blessings. When we remember to look up, we become aware of the beauty and blessings that surround us. Right before I go to sleep, I pray the Lord's Prayer and talk to God about my day: good things that I said or did. Then, I talk about things that I said or did that I wished I wouldn't have. I conclude by praying for friends and family members. My absolute favorite place to commune with God is while out in nature, whether it is on a walk at the park, gardening, or sitting in my back yard. For me, nature is a sacred and special place, where I can meet with God and also quiet my mind. If we wait for Him to respond, we will receive guidance for our lives as well as peace. Jeremiah 29:13 says, "And you will seek Me and find Me, when you search for me with all your heart." If you don't already have a practice, I encourage you to start. Converse with God. Your mind will be illuminated with visions, your heart lightened, and closed doors will open.

Blessed Scripture

And I will pray the Father and He will give you another Helper, that He may abide with you forever.

John 14:16

Prayer Notes

MY GUARDIAN ANGEL

*F*or as long as I can remember, I have wanted to be an actress. I loved watching old movies and musicals with my family as a kid. Some of the favorites were *The Music Man, Gigi, The Sound of Music,* and *Some Like It Hot.* I would just get lost in these stories; they were full of romance and adventure: a complete escape from everyday life. At school during recess, my classmates and I would recreate scenes from our favorite movies or television series, the most memorable being *The Wizard of Oz.*

One of my favorite television shows was *"The Dean Martin Show"*. I had a huge crush on Dean! He was my first invisible playmate. Much to my mother's amusement, when she would ask who I was going to play with in our backyard, I would usually respond Dean Martin. I had decided at a very early age that one day I would be one of the Golddiggers on his show. The Golddiggers were a group of singers and dancers who performed in very sparkly costumes. I recall a lot of sequins and GoGo boots. Sadly, I did not become a Golddigger, but my parents did buy me a few wigs and a great pair of GoGo boots.

I took voice lessons and a variety of dance lessons ranging from ballet, tap, jazz, pointe, disco, and Polynesian. As I mentioned before, my mom used to sing with an acting group from Salem United Church of Christ. My mom, siblings, and I would perform every summer in two to three plays with this group for almost a decade. We loved being around our theatre friends. As a young adult, I had received my B.A. in Drama from Loyola University and my dream had changed as I now wanted to move to New York and perform on Broadway.

I had quit my job and was making a living acting locally by performing on stage and in commercials when I discovered that I was pregnant. My boyfriend was my leading man in the play that we had just opened. Although I loved him, I realized that I wasn't in love with him. I knew that if we married, we would be divorced within the year. I thought that my best option would be to raise my child on my own with the assistance of family and friends. One of the hardest things that I had to endure in my life was telling my mom and grandma that I was pregnant. I had panic attacks worrying how they would receive the news. I kept rehearsing scenarios of how that conversation was going to play out. I had morning sickness that would last the entire day, so I knew that I would have to tell them sooner rather than later. A few weeks passed, and then I shared my secret. My mom handled the news better than my grandma. There were so many emotions, but we talked through everything. The point is: we got through this with love and understanding. Once my baby arrived, they adored her!

With a baby on the way, I needed more income and acquired a job with a national chain selling jewelry, gloves, hats, and a treasure trove of other accessories. The shop was located in the Jax Brewery in the French Quarter.

I have always loved working in the French Quarter. There are an abundance of art galleries, lovely dress shops, unique jewelry stores, and some of the finest restaurants in the world. My favorite restaurant is Irene's with its delicious Italian fare, lovely courtyard, and charming piano bar. I always feel like I have been transported back to Italy while dining in its cozy rooms. If you are ever in New Orleans, you should check it out.

This new shop that I chose to work in seemed to attract shoplifters. It seemed like almost every week, we would have to call security. Sometimes the security guards would share stories of those they caught. One lady turned out to be very wealthy, but was having marital issues and was using this as a way to get her husband's attention. Some of the shoplifters were just desperate people doing whatever they could to survive.

We had some shoplifters who would come in on a consistent basis. One of our regulars would sneak in, tear off the price tags, and then bring the merchandise to the register and ask for a refund. We even had a few brazen customers who would try to remove the security tags right in front of our cameras.

Every day on my way to work, I would wonder what the day's drama would be. Who would our shoplifter be today? Which salesperson would be accused of stealing someone else's sale? It was always something.

I had started working at this shop right after I had become pregnant, but they were very particular with their rules and we were not allowed to sit down during our shifts unless we were on break in the stockroom. I was very fortunate to work with a genuinely caring Assistant Manager, who would always bring a chair out for me to sit on during my shift. Ruby was awesome! Her warmhearted nature helped me through this trying time. While I was working there, during the course of my pregnancy, I went from being a petite girl of 5'2" and weighing 110 pounds to weighing 172. My feet became so swollen that the only shoes I could wear were bedroom slippers. Can you imagine? All dressed up for work with pink bedroom slippers on my feet!

Almost once a week, while assisting customers, I would break into tears and say, "I'm not fat, I'm pregnant", to which many would pat me on the back and tell me that they knew that. Some were empathetic and comment that everything would be okay. Some of the customers would feel so badly for me that they would end up purchasing something. I did not intend for this to become a selling strategy. I was a hormonal and emotional wreck! Even though I was an unwed mom-to-be, I was very excited about welcoming my baby to our world. She was due to arrive in early August, and I was truly delighted about this new chapter in my life that was about to begin.

One day while at work, I was asked to go to the stockroom and retrieve an item from the top shelf. The stockroom was always a mess. It was overcrowded with clothes, gloves, tights, hats, hatboxes, among an assortment of other accessories. There were boxes stacked precariously upon other boxes. I mentally prepared myself for this challenge and then I began my journey up the ladder. I was on the upper rung as I began to search through the boxes. Suddenly, to my dismay, the boxes began to slip. I tried desperately to hold some with my right hand while trying to push some of them back with my left hand. It was no good! I had completely disturbed the manner in which they were placed. I knew that within a few moments they were all going to tumble and I would be knocked to the ground with them. I said in a meek, panic filled voice," Oh dear God, please help me!". I had no sooner uttered these words, when next to me on my left side, a huge angel appeared.

He was at least seven feet tall and extremely muscular with long, curly blonde hair that hung slightly above his shoulders. His body was horizontal next to mine and I could hear the flapping of his wings although I couldn't see them. His robe was a dazzling shade of white, and I could see all the colors of the rainbow in it. His robe had a prism effect, just like the tunnel that I saw in heaven. He grabbed me with his right hand and pushed everything that was falling back into place with his left. I felt so tiny next to him. He gently placed me on the ground and then vanished.

I sat down at our small lunch table and tried to compose myself before heading back to the sales floor empty handed. A few minutes later, a co-worker came in and asked," Are you alright? You look like you have seen a ghost." I smiled and thought to myself, "No not a ghost, an angel". I replied that I was fine and that I would be back out on the sales floor shortly. I was intensely shaken up, yet I was incredibly grateful that God had sent this amazing angel to help me. This experience is another that confirmed what I knew to be true: God is near and desires to help us when we call out to Him.

My Guardian Angel Scripture

For He shall give His angels charge over you,
To keep you in all your ways.
In their hands they shall bear you up,
Lest you dash your foot against a stone.

Psalm 91:11-12

Prayer Notes

THE VISIT

$\mathcal{I}$n 1991, I was expecting my first child. As a single mom-to-be, my head was spinning with all sorts of questions. I mainly wondered if I would be a good parent. I was worried that I wouldn't know when I was in labor as compared to false labor. How does one know exactly what a baby wants when he is crying uncontrollably? What on earth do I name him?

Eventually, I had a name picked out for a son, but once I shared with family and friends what that name was, they all started praying that I would have a daughter. The name that I had chosen for my son was Atticus Ezekiel. They all said that I would ruin the child's life if I named him that. Some of my friends said that he would be tormented by fellow classmates and given terrible nicknames. Only one of my friends liked the name, and every time I saw Mickey, he would bend down to my stomach and say, "Hey there Atticus, old buddy. How are you doing in there?" The fact is that I loved the name then, and I am still quite fond of it today. The name Ezekiel comes from the Bible and he was a wonderful Old Testament prophet. I realize now that the combination of those two names is a bit much. Today if I was faced with the challenge of naming my son, I would choose either Joseph or Michael for a middle name.

The reason that I chose this name is because the character Atticus Finch from *To Kill A Mockingbird* had always reminded me of my father and my childhood. Even though, my dad had passed away when I was only seven years old, he left behind so many strong and wonderful memories. Two years after Dad lost his fight to cancer, my fourth-grade class was required to read *To Kill A Mockingbird*. Atticus's morals and his incredible love for his children were the qualities that he shared with my father.

Dad had a remarkable resemblance to the actor Yul Brenner, so much so that people would stop him on the street and ask him for his autograph. He would sign his own name and then pose with both of his hands firmly on his hips like Yul in *The King and I*. Some people would comment, "Oh, Yul Brenner must be your stage name". Nonetheless, his true character reminded me of Atticus. Dad worked as an auditor for a bank, and no matter how tired he was when he came home, he found time to spend with us. He had taught me how to read and write before I started school. He would always ask how our day was and wanted to know how we spent it.

They evenings would oftentimes find us singing and dancing around the piano, and there were endless games and piggyback rides. The house that we shared was charming and cozy. Before bedtime, Dad would finally have an opportunity to relax in his green and white upholstered chair in the living room. I would grab my blue prayer book with decorative flowers that he and mom had given me, and we would pray together. I still have the little blue prayer book on my bookcase, and it is one of my most cherished possessions. After prayer time, he would pick each one of us up and toss us into bed. Like literally toss us from the end of the bed. Several times we hit our heads on the headboards, but we didn't care. The delight that we experienced on our short flight before landing made up for the few head bumps. Sometimes, we would gleefully shout, "Hey Dad, do it again" as we lined up at the foot of the bed with the anticipation of being tossed one more time.

Unfortunately, I couldn't convince a soul what a fabulous name it was and seriously began praying that I would be able to choose a girl's name that wouldn't cause her any trauma.

One evening, as I was sitting on one of our over-stuffed chairs in the den and thinking intensely about little girl names, I had a most unusual visit. Standing next to me on my left side and about three feet away was St. Joseph and an angel of the Lord's. The angel was to St. Joseph's left and standing slightly behind him. St. Joseph was bathed in white light. He was a lot shorter than what I would have expected. His hair and beard were white, and he had crystal blue eyes and an olive complexion. As he spoke, he held his hands in front of him and gestured frequently. He announced himself to me and I had no fear of being with him, but the angel kept drawing my attention. He was tall with brown, shaggy hair, and his eyes were dark, yet filled with life. It looked as though there were flames of fire dancing in them. He was dressed in a white robe and had a sword attached to his left hip. I was fascinated!

St. Joseph went on to tell me that I was going to have a daughter and that I was to name her Madeleine for two reasons. The first reason was that she was to be named after St. Mary Magdalene, and I was to go forth and sin no more. The second reason was that it would go very nicely with my husband's last name. Since I wasn't married, I took this as a promise from God that one day, I would be. I happily replied, "Okay", meaning that I would honor his message. He bowed his head slowly in agreement and disappeared the same way he came.

A few weeks later, I was looking through a St. Joseph's Bible that listed the saints and their feast days, hoping that this would help me choose her middle name. I discovered a St. Madeleine Sophie, who was the founder of the Society of the Sacred Heart of Jesus. I thought that it was a pretty name, and I liked the idea that she would be named after two saints. I looked up the meaning for both names and learned that Madeleine means elevated, from on high, and Sophie means wise. I finally felt at peace about her name and just prayed that when the time came, her delivery would be an easy one.

Several months later, I delivered a precious baby whose name is, of course, Madeleine Sophie. We call her Madee. Today, she is a very beautiful and extremely smart young lady. She has truly been a blessing to me, and I can't imagine what my life would have been like without her.

The next part of this story is painfully honest, but the story would not be complete without it. So as distressing as this information is, I feel that I am to share it with you. After Madee was born, I re-met an old friend from college, Vince, and we began dating. It didn't take us too long to realize that we were in love, and we began talking about getting married. In the beginning of our relationship, I was obedient to what God had asked of me, refraining from sex, but the more time we spent together, the closer we became emotionally and ultimately, sexually. Several months later, instead of getting married, we broke up. It was a heartbreaking experience for both of us. We remained friends and even tried dating again a few years later.

It was at this later moment in time, that I realized we were meant to be in one another's lives for a season. We were not destined to be together forever.

My rationalization for sharing this is that when you enter into an agreement with God, it is not to be taken lightly. God expects us to keep our promises when we make them, no matter how difficult that may seem. When God sends us on a mission, He expects us to be obedient and faithful. It is only then that we can receive our reward for honoring Him.

Looking back over my life and all the fears that I had while I was expecting, I have come to understand the two most important things that we can do for our children: to spend as much time as we can with them and to let them know how dearly they are loved. Children need love and encouragement in order to develop their potential to the fullest. They need to be bold in the pursuit of their dreams. I have also learned that God is easily accessible. His love for us is unconditional,and if we ask for guidance and wisdom, He will truly show us the way.

The Visit Scripture

Ask and it will be given to you; seek and you will find; knock, and it will be opened to you. For everyone who asks receives, and he who seeks finds, and to him who knocks it will be opened.

Matthew 7:7-8

Prayer Notes

HEAVENLY MUSIC

*O*ne afternoon, as I sat at my grandmother's kitchen table, God blessed me in a unique way. My grandmother sat opposite me, reading the newspaper as my mom was scurrying about the kitchen preparing lunch. Vince and I had recently broken up, and I wasn't handling it very well. Vince was the old friend from college that I began dating when Madee was one month old. We hadn't seen each other in years and re-met at a mutual friend's party. We truly enjoyed one another's company, and he asked for my number before I left that evening. He called me about a week later and we had a wonderful first date that began an intense love affair. When he picked me up for our first date, he met Madee, and was reintroduced to my mom and grandma. We went to a movie, where we shared popcorn and snowcaps. Toward the end of the movie, he reached for my hand. There were definitely sparks flying as the movie lit up our faces while we held hands in the dark. After the movie, he took me dancing at a club that had a live band that played Glenn Miller style music. We were the youngest couple there. For one of the songs, we were trying to copy the dance moves of the other dancers and not succeeding. A few older people laughed and yelled, "Hey, you are not doing that right." We laughed back and replied, "We know!" The date was polished off by going to an old dive bar whose jukebox included Dean Martin and Frank Sinatra's music. He told me a few weeks later that he knew he was in love with me even before our first date.

A little shy of a month into our dating relationship, I performed at a benefit show for my dear friend Freddy who had recently passed away and who had given so much to the theater community with his musical talent. After the performance, Vince and I had gathered with friends and audience members in the theater's courtyard before heading back to my home. As Vince finished his cigarette on the sidewalk right outside the theater with smoke circling his head, he said, "Tonight's the night." I inquisitively asked, "Oh yeah? Tonight's the night for what?" He responded, "Tonight's the night we elope." I was completely surprised! At first, I agreed, but then quickly changed my mind. I didn't want to elope. A friend of mine from work had eloped, and she said that her and her husband never felt like they were really married.

They divorced a short time later. So, even though I didn't want to elope, we spoke of getting married and went ring shopping a few times. As you may recall from the previous story, that instead of getting married, we sadly broke up a few months later.

My heart was completely broken. I wasn't eating or sleeping. He was one of the greatest loves of my life! At the time I was twenty-seven years old and was engulfed in a sea of depression. By this time, I had lost all of the weight that I had gained during the course of my pregnancy and then some. I sat gazing downward in a state of despair wondering about my life and the direction I was headed in. Then, I heard the most beautiful music. The music was classical with a sweet melody; most importantly, it had the ability to lift my spirits. I no longer felt the heaviness of the despair. It gave me goose bumps. I looked up at my mom and grandma and then around the room to see where the source was. I asked them if they heard the music also. They both looked at me quizzically and said no. They went on to say that maybe what I heard was coming from outside since I was sitting closest to the door. The music had become distant while I was speaking to them, so I silently agreed with them, shrugged my shoulders, and rested my head in my hands as I gazed downward.

A few moments later, I heard it again - loud and clear. I looked up and said, "There it is again. Don't you hear it?" They looked at me like I was nuts and said, "No dear." This time, as I glanced about the room trying to discover where the music was coming from, I happened to look above my head and there they were: two little cherubs over my head. They looked like sweet, chubby, naked babies and they resembled cherubs from Renaissance paintings. They had strawberry blonde, curly hair and wore the sweetest expressions on their faces. Their bodies were draped in white, flowy fabric. One of them held a small, gold harp and the other one was holding a gorgeous box that music played from. The box was pale blue with ivory carvings of angels on it and was trimmed in gold. It was a cylinder-shaped box about six inches tall. The top of the box came to a point with a small, gold ball at the top. The doors on the music box opened and closed as the music played. I started smiling and was filled with total joy. I looked over at my grandmother and my mom to see if either of them could see the cherubs or hear this incredible music. Since they both continued with their previous chores, I knew that they could not. My spirit was immediately lifted by the little angels. This experience allowed my heart and soul to begin to heal. God had intervened in my deep depression and had sent His angels to cheer me up. The cherubs were a source of hope. Their presence had the power to change the atmosphere of my heart. During this difficult time of brokenness, I had pressed heavily into God searching for answers and healing. I wasn't healed immediately by the presence of the cherubs, but I knew that God had heard my prayers and that in time, my heart would mend.

Heavenly Music Scripture

Let everything that has breath praise the Lord.
Praise the Lord!

Psalm 150:6

Prayer Notes

MADEE'S ANGELS

*I*n the homes that I grew up in, my parents' and my grandparents', supernatural events would happen every so often. There were occasions of empty boxes flying across the floor, the piano playing, and a hallway light switching on by itself. The hallway light coming on by itself started happening after one of my Grandma's nurses, Estelle, whom we adored, passed away after being involved in a car accident. When that light would come on, I would feel an instant peace and think that Estelle was watching over us.

One night when my daughter was about two years old, I experienced a phenomenon. I had tucked her into her crib, pulled up the side of her bed, and left her to her dreams. I then rejoined the rest of the family in the breakfast room for dessert. About an hour later, we heard Madee crying at the top of her lungs. As my grandmother and I ran to the doorway of her room, we became frozen by fear. Our feet felt like they had become glued to the floor, and we literally could not move. It was though there was a force field holding us in place that we could not pass through.

What we saw was that somehow the side of her bed had come unlatched and had slipped down. Madee was standing in the middle of her bed crying, and her little body was teetering back and forth. She was about to fall over the side of the bed onto the hard, terrazzo floor and we were physically powerless to help her. I began to pray silently. A few seconds after I began to pray, a beautiful angel appeared in front of her. The angel was about six feet tall with long, dark, brown hair and tremendous wings. The expression of her face was soft, with incredible blue eyes adorning the rest of her features. There was an air of dignity and compassion about her. Her back was toward Madee and she was facing my grandmother and me. Her arms were outstretched from side to side to protect Madee from falling. As soon as she appeared, I felt at peace. I knew that everything was going to be alright. It amazes me how fast prayers are answered sometimes. Then, about a minute later, the angel said sweetly, but with a little attitude, "Do you mind coming to get your baby? I have other things that I have to do." "Oh, yes," I replied, awakening out of my daze. I was now able to move, and I quickly crossed the room to my daughter. As I reached her bed and held my arms out to grab her, the angel disappeared. I held Madee tightly in my arms and thanked God for His love and protection.

This was not the only time that I would see one of Madee's guardian angels. Many years would pass, then when she was about seven years old, I saw one in her bedroom late at night. We had transformed my grandma's sewing room into Madee's new bedroom. There was an adorable mural on her wall with a tree, flowers, and a large sun. Her ceiling was painted a light blue with a few clouds. One evening while she was sleeping, I quietly snuck into her room to put away some of her clothes. The dresser sat to the left of the doorway and on the other side of the dresser, were two nice sized closets. Her bed was on the opposite wall from the closets and dresser.

I quietly entered her room and was about to open one of the dresser's drawers, when I was startled by an angel on the other side of the dresser. He was about 5'9" with tanned skin and curly, golden blonde hair that fell about two inches below his shoulders. He had a very youthful face and appeared to be no more than about twenty years old.

I must have startled him as well because he drew his sword on me. I just kept saying over and over, " I am her mom. I am just her mom. " He put his sword away, and I finished putting her clothes away. I looked over at my daughter who was still sleeping peacefully as I left the room.

That would be the only time that I saw this angel. However, I used to think that he was in her room every night watching over her. It is comforting to know that there are heavenly angels who look over us to guard us in our most vulnerable moments.

Madee's Angels Scripture

Take heed that you do not despise one of these little ones, for I say to you that in heaven their angels always see the face of My Father who is in heaven.

Matthew 18:10

Prayer Notes

SAVED

*O*n September 21, 1995, I was headed to Baton Rouge. It was late at night and I was to drive about an hour and a half to meet my aunt and uncle at their home. My aunt had invited me on a weekend retreat in Arkansas and we would be leaving Baton Rouge very early the next morning with a group of six ladies total. As I was driving to their home, I started thinking about how excited I was about this weekend; I thought of it as a mini-vacation. This was the third time that my Aunt Rose had invited me on one of these retreats, but it was the first one that I had agreed to go on. Everything was going so wonderfully in my life in New Orleans. I was working at a jewelry store in the French Quarter and my acting career was going very well. I was also dating someone special and most importantly, spending quality time with my daughter Madee, who was four at the time. Yet with all these wonderful things going on in my life, I felt led to journey to Arkansas.

It was close to eleven o'clock p.m. when I arrived at my relatives' home. I sat up talking to my aunt, uncle, and my cousin Gabby, who has always seemed more like a sister than a cousin. When we were growing up, Aunt Rose and Uncle Charlie were always so full of life and took such an interest in my brother, sister, cousins, and myself. They made us feel valued. Uncle Charlie was never too busy to spend time with us and concocting games to keep us amused. Aunt Rose was always ready at a moment's notice to listen to any problem and offer great insight. She also taught us to dance while listening to the Beatles singing "I Want to Hold Your Hand" on her bright kitchen floor.

After my cousin left and my uncle retired for the evening, Aunt Rose tried to prepare me for our trip. She told me that the retreat would be very different from the ones I had been on in the past. She informed me that this was a non-denominational retreat and that I was going to see things that I had never experienced before. She told me about people resting in the Spirit, what it meant when people held their hands certain ways- one way, testifying and the other giving everything up to God and she told me about speaking in tongues. While I sat there listening to her, I realized that I was in way over my head. I didn't understand many of the terms that she was using, I didn't totally grasp the idea about being a born-again Christian, and I thought dear God, what have I gotten myself into?

At this point I think Aunt Rose noticed the lost look that I had written all over my face and she asked me in her sweet, quizzical way, "If you were to die tonight, do you know where you would be spending eternity? I replied, "Well, I don't think that I have done anything really wrong; I've been pretty good. I've never killed anyone or anything like that, so I would assume that I would be going to heaven." She looked at me and said very assuredly, "I know where I'm going when I leave this earth." Now I was intrigued! I asked her how she could know without a doubt where she would spend eternity. She said that when she became a born-again Christian, she accepted Jesus into her life and believed that He is God's only son who was crucified for our sins and raised from the dead. It is only in believing in Him through faith and God's grace that we enter God's heavenly kingdom. She explained that our good works account for nothing if we don't have a relationship with Jesus. She gave me plenty to think about as I lapsed into sleep.

The next morning, we left on an eight-hour ride to Arkansas and when we arrived, there was a noticeable change in the weather; it was much colder in Hot Springs than New Orleans! We checked in at this beautiful 520-acre ranch where we stayed in bunkhouses out in the woods. After unloading the van, we accompanied about four hundred other ladies for dinner. We were well fed, and I was greatly anticipating what was to come this first night of our journey. During dinner, I was introduced to a friend of my aunt's from her church that didn't ride up with us. Her name was Nancy and we immediately became friends. She became very important to me on this trip, because I was able to talk to her about things that I couldn't talk to my aunt about such as romantic situations. After dinner we moved into the main meeting room, which seemed more like a gymnasium that was extensively decorated. The stage had a replica of a big city and on one side there was a pillar of cloud and on the other was a pillar of fire. The lights dimmed, and the lady who runs Sun Valley Ranch- Dottie Mae- made a very dramatic entrance. I was very skeptical as I listened intensely to this little Godly woman, who was full of wisdom and spoke with a precious Southern twang. She reminded me of Vickie Lawrence's character from the television show, "Momma's Family".

As I sat there, the Lord showed me in a vision, that I had built up a wall around myself. The wall was built out of bricks made from grudges that I held onto from many years beforehand. These past hurts that I couldn't let go of had caused me to let certain people out of my life and I'm sure that they never really knew why we weren't friends any longer. I realized that somewhere along my path, I had stopped being that happy, free-spirited person I was and had traded my joy for a prison of grudges and disappointments. I felt extremely alone even though I was surrounded by four hundred women. I controlled my emotions outwardly, although tears welled up in my eyes as I sat there silently praying for God to change my heart and to show me the way. It was a simple prayer, but it made all the difference in the world. As I prayed, I saw the wall crumbling and for the first time in years, I felt free.

I returned my attention back to Dottie Mae who was praying over various people near the stage. There was one woman up there who I later found out was eighty years old. While Dottie Mae was praying over her, she fell down and was resting in the Spirit. This was the first time that I had ever witnessed anything like this, and I became panicky because I thought she had had a heart attack. I leaned over to my aunt and kept asking her if the woman was alright. She said that she was and that she would never be the same once she was up. Several minutes had passed and the woman was still lying on the floor, and then finally one of her friends went over and sat by her side. A few moments later, with the help her friend, she was up and fine. Actually, she was more than fine- she was literally glowing, and I knew that for her something spectacular had just happened.

It was getting very late and Dottie Mae was closing for the night, but she said that she would stay with her team as long as necessary for all those who wished to be prayed over. I turned to Aunt Rose and said that I wanted to go up for prayer. To say the least, she was shocked! I went up to the edge of the stage, and my aunt stood right behind me speaking in tongues. I was very nervous! I stood there trembling not sure what to expect and as fate would have it, Dottie Mae was the person who prayed over me. She just placed her hand on my shoulder and began to pray and I closed my eyes. The next thing that happened was most unusual. It was if the Holy Spirit was giving me mouth to mouth resuscitation. I felt extremely light-headed as I realized that God himself was breathing new life into me. As I left the gymnasium to head back to the bunkhouse, I was so blissful, I felt lighter, and looked forward with great expectation to see what the new day would bring.

The next morning came quickly, but there is nothing like waking up in the country. I woke up feeling exhilarated. I felt that I had a fresh start and that anything was possible. After breakfast, Dottie Mae plowed right on with her teaching on the Holy Spirit. Before we broke for lunch, we were given an unusual gift- a drainpipe. It was to represent the Holy Spirit raining down on us His joy and love. Dottie Mae told each of us to find a spot on the hill where we could eat lunch alone and then imagine the drainpipe as a connection to God in which the Holy Spirit could minister to us.

It was an absolutely gorgeous day, and after I finished my lunch, I decided to go for a long walk by myself. As I was walking along the hillside, I saw these pretty yellow wildflowers that reminded me so much of my father and our long, hot summers that were spent on my Uncle Woody's farm in Mississippi. My memories of my dad have always been very vivid. He was simply wonderful; he was a kind, gentle man with a quiet spirit and a warm laugh. As I walked on, I passed one of the lakes on the property where I paused for a moment; it was there that I heard the Lord calling my name. This in itself was wonderful, but it was the phrase that followed that caused worry and confusion. What I heard was, "Eva …watery grave". I heard it several times and quickly decided to move far away from the water and to continue down the hill.

I finally came to rest by another lake, where I sat down by the water's edge and contemplated everything that I had heard over the last two days. I had known Jesus my entire life, however on this trip I realized just how selfishly I had lived; that I hadn't been following Him but living by my own standards. I realized that I had accepted whatever I was taught in church instead of reading God's word for myself and meditating on it. I had come to believe that God felt differently about certain issues than He had during Biblical times.

Earlier that afternoon, I had spoken with Nancy about many topics- including sex. Any question I had or any statement that I tried to defend by my own reasoning was quickly shot down by a friend wielding a Bible. She would simply say, "That's not how God feels about that subject". She would efficiently find a Bible passage, hand it to me and say, "Here, read this". I would read whatever she handed me, give a horrified gasp, close the Bible and hand it back to her. I discovered that many of my views did not correspond with what God wanted for me. I also realized that if I chose to follow Christ there would be many things that I would have to give up. The question now was, did I want a new life and was I willing to give up those things that suffocated me on a spiritual level. All I could think about was the previous night when God had allowed me to see that wall crumbling about me and I felt like I was able to breathe. I felt free. It was a freedom from worries and fears – because He is always with me to guide me and give me strength; a freedom from denial- because no matter how fickle man's affections may be toward me, God's love for me is true. He knows all my faults and loves me completely in spite of them. I worried how my friends would feel toward me if I chose this new path that was before me. Then I grasped the fact that I couldn't go on with my life the way it had become especially after tasting a new one; one that was full of promise and peace. It was at this moment that I decided to pick up my cross and follow wholeheartedly after the Lord.

That evening turned out to be one of the most memorable in my life. We were taken on a hayride to a distant section of the property. When we got off the truck, we each had to pick a number out of a bowl. The number placed one in a prayer group and allowed you to meet and pray for other people that you didn't come with. Dottie Mae led us in an incredible exercise as we sat on the grass in a circle as we waited for our dinner to finish cooking. Dottie Mae was going to show us through this exercise that God is everywhere and that He can speak to all of us at the same time yet have a very different message for each of us. Each group had a leader that led us in a brief prayer and then we were instructed to close our eyes, be very still, and wait on the Lord. This experiment lasted ten minutes, ten minutes of complete silence, where every lady heard the Lord speak to her personally. Some heard the Lord's voice, some saw visions, some had messages for someone in the circle, but everyone was ministered to. After the ten minutes were over, we each shared something that the Lord showed us during that time. What I learned was that God is indeed omnipresent and omnipotent and that this world that we live in is so busy and noisy that it can drown out His voice. However, if we find a quiet place and seek Him with our whole heart, we will hear from Him.

Later that evening, we went back to the gymnasium, where they had prepared some skits for us. Then everyone participated in worshipping the Lord through music and dance. One of the songs that night was "River of God". Dottie Mae even had a section of the stage rigged up so that water could rain down upon us. Everyone was having a fabulous time, when Dottie Mae announced that even though it was pretty late, all those who wanted to continue worshipping could do so. Then she added that one of the ladies asked if she could be baptized in one of the lakes on the property. Dottie Mae had said yes and offered to everyone the same opportunity. She said that she wanted those people who had made a decision to give their lives to Christ, to read Romans 8:1-11 ten times before going to bed. It states, "There is no condemnation for those in Christ Jesus..." She really wanted us to plant that scripture in our hearts. I knew then why the Lord had called my name earlier that day by the lake and followed it with the phrase "watery grave". I obeyed God and told my aunt about my decision to be baptized in the morning. She was totally amazed and very excited that the Lord had used her during this crucial time in my life. I went back to our cabin, read Romans 8:1-11 ten times, and tried my best to prepare for the coming day.

I could barely sleep. I flew out of bed the next morning and raced down the hill by the lake. There were fourteen of us that had decided to be baptized and I sat there patiently while my aunt and new friends prayed for me. It was so cold out that morning, but Dottie Mae had prayed that the water would be comfortable and surprisingly, it was fine. The idea of baptism is that you are burying the person that you are- all your old ways of dealing with issues are passed away as you go down under the water, and when you arise you are never the same again. In baptism, we identify with Jesus' death and when we come forth from the water we relate to His resurrection. Our "old man" has passed away and we are raised to walk in newness of life. It is truly a transformation! Your whole life and attitude changes when you accept Jesus as your Lord. For me becoming a born-again Christian gave me strength. When I start to think negatively or when those "what ifs" creep into my mind, I set them free and focus my attention on God. No matter what comes, He is right there with me helping me through. Many of our worries stem from anticipating future events. Many of these events will never happen and if they do, God is walking right beside us. Holding our hands and guiding us along the pathways.

The first person that I saw get baptized was the eighty-year-old lady that I thought had a heart attack on our first night at Sun Valley Ranch. This was one of the most beautiful moments that I had ever witnessed. This lovely older lady giving herself to the Lord and stating that no matter how many days she had left she would follow Him. When my time came, I joined Dottie Mae and one of her employees in the lake and while I was trying to hold back my tears of joy, I made a public declaration that I accepted Jesus as my Lord and Savior. Dottie Mae said a prayer over me and I was completely emerged in the water. When I came up, I felt wonderful! I felt as though I had been given a second chance to grab hold of life and live it to the fullest, but to live according to God's rules and not my adaptation of them.

I was so full of joy, that when I made it back to work, I didn't have to say a word about what had happened because my co-workers could see the outward change in me. Some friends even said it looked like I was walking on air and that is exactly how I felt.

If you are going through life feeling burdened and overwhelmed, you are missing out and you don't have to. It is amazing to me how my life changed so dramatically and wonderfully in one weekend! The change came when I decided to leave my old burdens behind and to enter the arms of love. Jesus is waiting for you with His arms outstretched and all you have to do is believe in Him. He will grant you great peace, joy, and rest from this world that can at times leave you so weary. If you are without a savior, I invite you to meet mine. Believe, pray this prayer and mean it with all of your heart, and watch how Jesus can change your life.

Lord Jesus, I come to you as a sinner in need of a savior. I repent of my sins, I release my past, and I turn to You. Please give me a new life and a pure heart. I believe that You died for me, and that Your blood pays for my sins and provides me with the gift of eternal life. By faith I receive that gift and acknowledge You as my Lord and Savior.

Saved Scripture

There is therefore no condemnation to those who are in Christ Jesus, who do not walk according to the flesh, but according to the Spirit.

Romans 8:1

Prayer Notes

GOD OF WONDERS

The pastor silenced the church by gaining everyone's attention when he announced, "Everyone be quiet. God is going to make Himself known!"

It was about two years after I was saved that I found a church home, The Abundant Life Fellowship. This was a wonderful non-denominational church! The pastor and associate pastors were awesome! The messages were always captivating and I left church full of hope and inspiration, like I was on a natural high after attending service. I never left service feeling like I had been condemned or beaten up by the message. The sermons definitely made me contemplate where I stood on my life's journey and areas in need of improvement, but I never left church feeling hopeless.

There were a group of people who belonged to the prayer team. You could send in prayer requests and they would pray for your needs. I believe that these members were very godly because when I entered the sanctuary, a sense of peace would wash over me and I could feel God's presence abiding there. During my membership there, I decided to remain celibate and was reading my Bible every morning as an act of worship and to grow closer to God.

While I was a member, I joined the choir and had quite a few supernatural experiences. This is the church that I was attending when I saw the Holy Spirit appear one night during choir rehearsal. As time went on, we went from having a nice size choir of about twenty members to a praise team that consisted of two men and three ladies, myself included, and a small band.

One morning at the beginning of service, we were standing in our usual line up. The praise team was in the middle of the altar with the band to our left of us and the pastors on the left of the band. As we were singing, I heard God whisper into my right ear that we needed to be quiet because He was going to show up. My body froze with anticipation of what He was going to do. I stopped singing and waited. After a few moments, I became self-conscious because the rest of the choir continued singing. Also, I started thinking that the church members probably thought that I had forgotten the lyrics so I started singing again, but very quietly.

It wasn't a second later, when the pastor silenced the church by gaining everyone's attention when he announced, "Everyone be quiet. God is going to make Himself known!" Almost right after that God appeared directly in front of where the choir was standing. God has a towering presence. He appeared in the form of a pillar of cloud just like He did in the Old Testament when He led the Israelites through the wilderness.

While reading the book of Exodus, I always pictured the column of cloud to be tall but fairly narrow, much like the columns that adorn the façade of our homes in the South. God is so much bigger than that! He slightly hovered above the ground and was pretty close to touching the ceiling of the sanctuary. He was about nine feet wide and there was a lot of movement within the cloudy pillar.

I kept staring at Him in amazement. In hindsight, I should have bowed down, gotten on my knees and humbled myself, but I didn't move. I had my eyes glued on Him as I didn't want to miss anything by having my face on the floor. This lasted about five minutes and then He simply disappeared.

Our pastor lingered an instant longer and then said something like, "Well I guess that is it." The pastor moved on to the next part of the service without reflecting on the event. I am not sure if anyone but myself witnessed the Lord's marvelous demonstration. No one spoke about this occurrence. I assume that the pastor witnessed what I saw since he began speaking a moment after God dissipated. I was always nervous about asking the others what they saw – if anything. I was leery about talking to the other choir members about my experiences for fear they might think I was strange.

One night while out with the choir for dinner, I was about to share my story about how I was struck by lightning as a child. Instead, I asked the three friends that I was dining with if any of them had seen God. They looked about the table at each other and then one of them replied, saying that he had not seen God, but that God promised that he would reveal Himself to him in his old age before he dies.

I wish now that I would have shared my stories sooner with my family, friends, and unbelievers. Fear of being judged has held me back from speaking more boldly about my faith and my supernatural experiences. Fear has held all of us back at various times in our lives. It is time to shed the cloak of fear, that wraps us up in darkness; that hinders us from moving forward and helping others to become either more spiritual or the best version of themselves. Search for the light within you and let it shine. Don't let fear prevent you from your purpose in life. Go after your dreams and share your stories with others.

God of Wonders Scripture

And it came to pass, when Moses entered the tabernacle, that the pillar of cloud descended and stood at the door of the tabernacle, and the Lord talked with Moses.

Exodus 33:9

Prayer Notes

DIVINE PROTECTION

*I*n 1997, Liz, Madee, and I decided to take a vacation to North Carolina to visit Liz's fiance' who was working on a jobsite there for the summer. We had decided to drive and would stop the first night in Atlanta. Driving time should have been about seven and a half hours. It took us much longer. We stopped for gas breaks, bathroom breaks, and a dinner break at The Cracker Barrel. We love stopping at The Cracker Barrel on road trips. Yes, I realize that it isn't fancy, but it offers a sense of sweetness and Southern charm.

It was when we decided to look for a room for the night that we started having some issues. It was very late and everywhere we stopped seemed to be either booked up or too shady to stay there. We were absolutely exhausted! With tired eyes and fatigue from riding for so long, we were beginning to get anxious about where we would sleep for the night.

We finally found a hotel that we thought, "How bad can this be?" because we spotted a limousine in the back parking lot. We walked up to go inside the lobby, but it was off limits. We received our room key from a lady behind a glass window, who pushed the key through a little slot as she warned us to be careful. Her statement sent a little shock of alarm through my body.

We drove to the back parking lot and had to pass by the limo to get to our room. When we drove passed it, we realized that it was painted eggplant purple with graffiti covering it. There were several people surrounding it playing loud music and partaking in drugs. Our arrival hadn't gone unnoticed as someone shouted something at us. We didn't feel safe. We had chosen badly and yet instead of leaving, we continued to find a spot close to our room. We quickly dragged our luggage up to the second floor, locked the door behind, and looked out the window. Down below we saw four or five of the members from the limo crowd move closer to the hotel. They were looking up toward our room and shouting incoherently at us.

We were so scared and absolutely exhausted. We began moving furniture pieces to block the door and part of the window. We figured that by blocking the window, we would hear them breaking in and that it might give us a second to protect ourselves. I have no idea what our weapons would have been: maybe manicure scissors and some hairspray?

The three of us held hands and prayed. First, we thanked God that our time on the road had been safe and fun. Secondly, we asked him for protection from those below who wished to harm us. We prayed earnestly. We finally fell asleep in the same clothes we had been traveling in with the shouting continuing in the distance.

When we woke up the next morning, we were surprised that we had actually been able to get some rest. Liz said that she had a dream that there were two giant angels outside our door protecting us. In astonishment, I said I had the same dream. In my dream, they were about seven feet tall with swords drawn, ready to fight at a moment's notice. Possibly, having the knowledge deep within us that they were there, allowed us to rest.

Everything was quiet outside, and we hurriedly left the hotel. We were very hungry and in much need of coffee. We found a quaint diner with a cute, chatty waitress. She asked us where we were from, so we shared that we were from New Orleans just passing through on our way to North Carolina. Also, we recounted our prior evening at the motel. She knew the motel well and said that we were lucky to be alive.

God had protected us from whatever evil was intended. We left the diner and continued on our journey. We had a wonderful beach vacation, where we were able to fellowship with family and new friends and to bask in the sun.

Divine Protection Scripture

He who dwells in the secret place of the Most High shall abide
Under the shadow of the Almighty.
I will say of the Lord, "He is my refuge and my fortress,
My God, in whom I trust."

Psalm 91:1-2

Prayer Notes

MONEY FROM HEAVEN

When I was in my early thirties, I worked at a shop in the Quarter that sold amazing jewelry and masks from all over the world. It was called the Gossip Shop.

Some of the masks were very simple, made from leather and crafted to look like something the Man in Black wore from The Princess Bride. These masks cost $25. Naturally, the more detailed the mask, the higher the price. There were some that were very large and magnificent creations of art. Interior Designers and collectors would shop with us for that special conversation piece. Those masks sold between $3,000- $7,000.

There was one gentleman that came in during the Mardi Gras holidays and purchased one of our $5,000 mask that he wore on Mardi Gras day. These masks were intended more for decoration than to be worn, but to each their own.

We also had a variety of feathered masks and beautiful papier mache masks from Italy. I had purchased a few of these to decorate my own home. I still have a lovely white crescent moon with rosy cheeks in my bedroom. There was also another one that I bought for my sister for her new home. It was a woman's face with a much smaller man's face and body below her face. The man was holding the woman's face over his head, like he adored her. His body was wrapped in her hair. The torso is what you would hold to put the mask over your face if you decided to wear it. This mask was absolutely beautiful and was painted in white and gold.

For the most part, I loved working there. I met interesting people from all over the world. Also, the people I worked with were wonderful. We were like a small family. Most of the time, everyone got along pretty well.

I had also made friends with those who worked in the shops next to ours. There would be delightful lunches at Mr. B's and The Flaming Torch, a little Mexican restaurant. Our boss, Mr. Jerry, would treat us to fancy dinners at Arnaud's or cocktails at The Bombay Club. One of my favorite friends to dine with was Joe, who worked right next door at an upscale jewelry store. Joe was quite the character! He was extremely good looking, resembling a young Mickey Rourke. He wore his hair very high in a pompadour and was a little salty that his name wasn't Elvis.

I would work at the Gossip Shop during the day and then at night, I would walk down to one of the theaters for rehearsal for *A Streetcar Named Desire*. I was blessed to play Stella and the cast and director for this project were absolutely amazing. The director had commissioned Delfeo Marsailais, one of our fabulous local musicians, to compose an original score for our play.

I had worked at the Gossip Shop on and off for about five years when I felt that it was time for a career change. The owner had started selling some unsavory items that I hated ringing up and wrapping for the customers. I won't disclose what these items were, but I didn't want to be around them. I spoke to the owner about this, and he felt that they were a cute and inexpensive souvenir for tourists. I prayed quite a lot about this situation. I was worried about quitting and looking for another job that would allow me to take time off for my daughter and time to pursue my acting career.

While praying one night, God told me that if I quit my job, He would show me the money. I countered with, if You show me the money, I will quit my job. I know that I should have unequivocally put my trust in God without hindrance. However, quitting my job without something else waiting in the wings seemed very scary.

About a week after this conversation with God, the play opened to wonderful reviews. Two of my dear friends, Alice and Norm, came to see the play opening weekend. After the performance was over that night, we walked through the mall together to get to our cars. As we were walking on the first floor, my foot stepped on something a little bulky. I ignored it for a second and kept walking. However, I then felt like I was guided to turn around and to take a closer look as to exactly what it was that I had stumbled upon. It was a plain white envelope. I called to my friends, who walked on ahead not noticing that I had stopped. I picked the envelope up and to my astonishment it was loaded with cash.

I put the envelope in my bag and we located a security officer. I asked if anyone had reported losing an envelope with money. He enquired, "How much money?" I countered with, "No, I am not saying." He said that no one had reported any money missing. I replied, "Very well. I will call tomorrow to check with the management office to see if anyone had reported anything related to this incident."

I followed up the next day, and no one had reported the missing money. I held on to the cash for two months and would call the security office about once a week. It was a rather large amount, and I didn't want anyone to get fired for losing money that might belong to one of the shops. After two months passed, I quit my job at the Gossip Shop. With the money that was found, I paid off my bills and had enough left over to buy me a little time while looking for another job.

Once again God was faithful! I was able to start a new job closer to home, making more money, that allowed the freedom that I desired.

Money From Heaven Scripture

I traverse the way of righteousness
In the midst of the paths of justice
That I may cause those who love me to inherit wealth,
That I may fill their treasuries.

Proverbs 8:20-21

Prayer Notes

JESUS IS COMING

*I*n April of 2000, I went on a retreat to Sun Valley Ranch in Arkansas with my sister, Liz, who was saved, and one of my best friends, Lauren, who wasn't. I have known Lauren for many years and she is a woman of great character. She has never known a stranger due to the fact that she makes friends so easily. I can't recall a time when I have seen her angry, nor have I heard her raise her voice to anyone. In the twenty plus years that we have been friends, we have never had an argument. She is genuinely sweet, intelligent, and thoughtful. Before the retreat, if one was to ask her where she would be spending eternity, she probably would have replied, "Heaven." She would have been wrong.

The first night that we gathered with the other retreaters (about three hundred and twenty women) in the auditorium which is always beautifully decorated according to the theme. This session's theme was "He is Coming" which was about the second coming of Jesus and the Book of Revelation. As we stood in the back by our seats and the guests were mingling, something most unexpected happened: Jesus appeared before me. He was dressed in a white robe and His presence glowed with such intensity! He is of medium height and build, yet quite muscular. His long, dark brown hair ends just before reaching His shoulders. He has an olive complexion with beautiful blue eyes, and He has the brightest smile that I have ever known. He took my right hand in His and said, "Hi." I was awestruck. We just stood there smiling at one another as He continued holding my hand. He then said, "Well, I just came over to say hi. I have to go now to greet others." As He started to leave, He glanced over at Lauren who was standing on my right side. Then, He leaned into me and said, "Not one of mine." He turned away from her and then greeted my sister, who was standing to my left. He held my sister by her shoulders and looked directly into her face and said, "Hi, Liz." She didn't hear or see Him, but continued singing along to the music that was being played over the loudspeakers. He looked back at me over His left shoulder, shook His head, shrugged His shoulders, then smiled at me before taking two steps and then vanishing. The retreat had just begun and because of that moment, it was already one of the best experiences of my life.

As a slight departure from the story, I would like to say that I have been blessed to see Jesus several times in my life. Every time that I have seen him, he looks the same and wearing a white robe. He is very easy to be with. His smile draws me in. Even though I am excited to see Him, I am also at ease. He knows me better than anyone and I am free to be my authentic self. He has seen me at my best and worst. My friend Josie has also seen Jesus a few times. She describes Him the same way that I do with dark brown hair, blue eyes, olive complexion, and a medium muscular build. However, when she sees Him, He is dressed in blue jeans, a white tee, and flannel. His hair is in a man's bun. I believe that Jesus appears to people in various dress, but the basics are still the same. He is always welcoming and wanting to spend quality time with all of us.

The next day, I was able to spend some time alone with Lauren. She confided in me that she was going through some major problems in her life; she seemed to be carrying the weight of the world on her shoulders and she was crying as she spoke. She seemed confused and very restless. I told her that she didn't have to handle what she was going through by herself. If she could put her life into Jesus's hands, He would take care of all her needs. I also told her that if she decided to accept Jesus as her Lord and Savior, it didn't mean that she wouldn't have problems anymore, but He would give her a new strength to deal with anything that the world might throw at her. We were then called back into the meeting. As we took our seats, Jesus appeared to me a second time and told me to keep praying for her.

During our next break, Lauren decided to go into Hot Springs to enjoy some luxuries at one of the spas. At dinner, Liz and I met up with some new friends and asked them to please pray for Lauren. Our prayer was that she would come to know Christ and find peace in her life.

After dinner, we moved back inside for the next event. The team of people that work at Sun Valley Ranch had re-decorated the gym while we were on break and had cleared the center of the floor so that we could worship through singing and praise dancing. Lauren made it back in time and we were very relieved because it was quite dark out and the ranch is located up a mountain. The stage was now decorated with a huge throne on stage right; on stage left was a replica of the Ark of the Covenant. In the center of the stage, there was an image of Jesus riding a white horse and wearing the crown of many crowns, symbolizing that He is the King of Kings. Lauren and I joined the other ladies in worship. Liz decided to not partake in the praise dancing due to her pregnancy. Thus, the evening began on a high note.

We were then asked to take our seats as they prepared for communion. During this time, Dottie Mae, who owns SunValley Ranch, instructed that after we made our way to the altar, that we should return to our seats or find a quiet spot where we could be alone to contemplate the sacrifice that Jesus made for us. As the lights dimmed, a dancer entered to the music and a young man representing Jesus took his place behind the gifts. He remained there while everyone went up to receive the bread and wine. I felt like I had been invited to the Last Supper. This visual was extremely powerful! When I returned to my seat, I was all alone. Liz and Lauren had each chosen a spot near the rear of the gym. I was thankful for this serene moment where I began to meditate about Jesus and what my salvation had meant to me. It has been, without a doubt, the greatest gift that I have been given. As I go through the trials in this life, there is a great comfort in knowing that when I leave the earth, I will be truly at peace and in the presence of the Lord forever. My dear friend Freddie used to say that when you find yourself in times of trouble ask, "What does this matter in the light of eternity?" It always helps to put things into perspective.

As I sat there, I saw Jesus manifest near the stage area. He walked over to me, knelt beside me on one knee, and kissed my left cheek. Then disappeared. All of a sudden, Lauren came racing over to me and she was full of joy; her countenance had totally been transformed. She was glowing. Out of breath, she said, "You will never guess what happened to me. I had my leg propped up on a bench and was leaning over the bread and wine thinking about everything, my life and what you had spoken to me about earlier. While I was deep in thought, this man Jesus that all of you have been speaking of, came over to me and put His foot next to mine on the bench. I know this is going to sound crazy, but He was there with me." It seems that while she was praying, Jesus appeared to her as if He was saying, "Yes I'm here. Did you call?" At this time, I revealed to her what happened the night before when He didn't claim her as one of His. I told her that Jesus was knocking on her heart's door waiting to come in. However, He is a gentleman. He won't barge in. He must be invited.

Sunday was the last day of the retreat and it was on this day that Lauren gave her life to Christ. She hasn't been the same since. She now has a relationship with Jesus and has encountered peace and joy in her life. How would your life change if you were to place your trust in God? Are there things that have you in bondage or wrapped up in sin? Give it God. Lay it at His feet and watch miracles unfold in your world.

Jesus is Coming Scripture

For whoever calls upon the name of the Lord shall be saved.

Romans 10:13

Prayer Notes

MIRACLE

Several years ago, my grandma was admitted to East Jefferson General Hospital for heart failure. The first night that she was there, my family gathered around her and prayed. There were about sixteen of us who stood around her holding hands and praying. She was hooked up to several machines to monitor her progress and she wasn't doing very well.

During the night, one of the doctors came in and told us that Grandma probably wouldn't be with us much longer because her kidneys had started to fail. At that point, they said that only three family members could be with her at a time. My cousin Gabby, Liz, and I stayed with her for a while, crying and praying over her. She had been totally incoherent and hadn't spoken at all that night, when all of a sudden, she opened her eyes, recognized us, and said, "Listen, I want you two girls to take care of your mother, and Gabby, you take care of her too. If I look down from heaven, and see that she is being neglected, I'll come back and haunt you." We started laughing through our tears because she had always been an extremely feisty lady, and we knew that she was being serious. She said, "I'm not joking!" We replied, "We know!" She then lapsed back into a deep sleep and as we left there that evening, we didn't expect to see her again.

Our hearts were extremely heavy. Not so much that Grandma was dying, but mainly because we didn't think that she was going to heaven. She was a good woman who had helped to raise us and would do anything for us. However, like I said earlier, she was very feisty! She was a female Archie Bunker. She was decidedly opinionated, and God help you if you didn't follow her advice. I had actually witnessed her throwing grown men out of our home. Once when a gentleman friend of mine came over for the first time late at night, we were chatting in the kitchen and nibbling on some leftovers. Harry said, "I really like your home; it is very charming." My grandma, who was in the next room sitting in her wheelchair overheard his comment. She wheeled herself into the kitchen and said, "This is my house. They live with me." She then wheeled herself from the room. We just laughed. Harry purchased a house many years after this visit. On his first night there, he rode around in an office chair, going from room to room saying, "This is my house. They live with me."

My grandma was an amazing cook. Every night she would prepare a four-course dinner for us. On one particular evening when I was in high school, we were all sitting in our regular places for dinner and she was standing next to the table dishing out the mashed potatoes. I don't remember the reason any longer, but she was furious with my grandpa. She wasn't yelling, but she was really letting him have it. My grandpa just sat there with his head resting on his left hand staring up at her with this expression of love on his face. I kept thinking that he must speak up for himself; is he really just going to sit there and not say anything? About a minute later, Grandma looked over at him and said, "Do you have anything to say?" He replied, " You know Carrie, I just love you. That is all there is to it. I just love you!" Grandma started to blush and exclaimed, " Oh Carl!" She giggled, and that was the end of it. What a great example my grandpa set for us. The whole time, he was just standing strong and replying in love.

When my grandma was eleven years old she had converted to Catholicism and had a strong relationship with the Blessed Mother. Whenever she found herself in time of crisis, she called out to Mary for help. While we can learn a lot from the Blessed Mother, we shouldn't allow her to take the place of Jesus. He is our only Savior. After I was saved, many times at home I had tried to pray with her and anoint her with holy oil, and she would say things like, "What are you crazy? Get away from me with that stuff." She was at times difficult, but she was loved dearly.

Anyway, getting back to her hospital stay. The next afternoon, my Aunt Rose went to visit her and when she walked into the hospital room, she couldn't believe her eyes. There sat Grandma on the side of her bed with her legs swinging back and forth, eating a turkey sandwich. God is so faithful! He heard our pleas and completely healed her. He granted her three more years of a rich life.

A few weeks after she returned home, I had the toughest conversation with her. God had revealed to me that she wasn't going to heaven unless she would repent and change her ways. I told her very gently that I would rather she hate me in this life and go to heaven, than for her to love me and spend an eternity in hell. I explained that Jesus died for us and that it is through believing in Him and accepting Him as your Lord and savior that you are saved. She cried and said that she didn't know why I hated her so much that I would say that she was going to hell. She wanted to know what she had done that was so wrong that she wouldn't be rewarded eternal peace. I told her that I didn't hate her, but that I loved her very much and was concerned about her destiny. As far as what she was doing wrong, I told her to ask the Lord. She left the room sobbing, and I thought that our relationship would never be the same.

God calls us to be holy people. We are to love God with all of our heart, mind, and soul. To be in relationship with Him. Also, God calls us to love our neighbor as ourselves. Who is our neighbor? Everyone! We are to be at peace with everyone. In those times of struggles and unrest, where you might not agree with another's opinion or actions, try to resolve the conflict in a loving way. Try to edify one another. Heaven will be made up of people from all walks of life. People of every race and religion. Be open minded and loving and I think you will be amazed how God can transform your life.

That afternoon a miracle happened. She had spent a good part of the day locked in her room and she had an authentic encounter with God. She became an enlightened spirit. When she came forth, she was a grandmother of a much softer nature: more loving, more patient, and kinder. I was right when I had drawn the conclusion that we would never be the same. Our relationship grew stronger than it had been, and she began to invite me to pray with her and to anoint her with holy oil. She became a joy to be around. When she left us in 1999, there was a great peace for we knew that her suffering had ended and that she had entered the arms of God.

Miracle Scripture

Fear not, for I have redeemed you; I have called you by
your name; you are Mine.
Isaiah 43:1

Prayer Notes

JESUS IS THE KEY

One night as I lay sleeping, the Lord gave me a powerful vision. In the dream appeared a young, pregnant woman in shabby clothes with a shawl wrapped around her. I was intrinsically aware that she was unwed, but her betrothed stood behind her. Next to her stood her petite mother and rugged father. All of them spoke with an Irish accent.

The father who had a very kind face, had bought his daughter a special gift to bless her and to give her hope for a beautiful future. The daughter opened the gift and it was a lovely Celtic silver cross that stood about ten inches tall, but it looked like it was broken. The daughter was terribly upset that the cross had a crack running along the front right side. Her mother began to cry and was holding her face with her hands as she repeatedly said, "Oh take it away; it is a bad omen." The father was very calm and said, "Look, it is not broken. Let me show you how it works." He unhooked the cross from its heavy base and opened the cross where the crack was in the silver. He then pulled from the cross a map of the world, which he unrolled and placed on the table. There were four plastic pieces in the base that he removed and set them in the middle of the map. These pieces were very vibrant in the colors of red, yellow, blue, and green. When these pieces were in place, they formed a type of keyhole. There was also a tiny wooden sailboat with a white sail that was in the arm of the cross; the sailboat ran its course along the outside of the vibrantly colored pieces. Then the father pulled out the last piece of the puzzle. It was a carved wooden figurine of Jesus and He fit into the very center of the board into the keyhole. As the father locked Jesus into place, the tiny boat began to move about the map. He said to his daughter, "If you keep your eyes on Jesus, He will direct your path."

Isaiah 26:3 says, "You will keep him in perfect peace whose mind is stayed on You, because he trusts in You." Whenever I become anxious or fearful, I recite this to myself and remember that Jesus is the key. He is the key to my joy and my peace. He is my provider and my salvation. When I remember this, my peace is restored.

Jesus is the Key Scripture

Every good gift and every perfect gift is from above, and
Comes down from the Father of lights, with whom there is no variation or shadow of turning.

James 1:17

Prayer Notes

THE PERFECT DAY

*I*t was a chilly February morning and I was thrilled to have the day off. I had been single for some time and kept praying that I would meet someone special. It is nearly impossible to meet anyone new if you keep traveling in the same circles and doing the same thing day after day, so I had decided the night before that I wouldn't say no. On this particular morning, I promised myself that I would treat myself to lunch, a new dress, and that I would say yes to all invitations. I would be open to all the possibilities that this day held.

After my usual routine of enjoying a cup of coffee and reading my Bible, I got ready and headed to Magazine Street. For lunch, I decided to dine at Taqueria Corona. It is a very charming, neighborhood Mexican restaurant. The meals are absolutely delicious and they serve some of the best margaritas in town.

As soon as I entered, I spotted an old friend that I used to do theatre with, Josh. It had been years since we had seen each other. Josh was on his lunch break and we had a great time catching up before he had to go back to work. I finished my meal which consisted of a yummy bean burrito topped with sour cream and a variety of spicy sauces and went to pay my bill. I was informed that Josh had secretly bought me lunch. How sweet!

The next stop was Fairy, an amazing shop with vintage inspired clothing, hats, shoes, and jewelry. It was owned by my dear friend Bella. Bella loves champagne and we partook of mimosas while I tried on various garments. Her shop was fabulous! It unfortunately closed a few years ago when Bella decided that it was time to switch careers and began selling real estate. After an hour and half of mimosas and trying to decide between what I wanted and needed, I purchased one dress and headed back home.

When I returned home, I shared stories of my day with my mom. As we were chatting, I received a phone call from Lauren who invited me to have a late lunch with her. I had already eaten, but since I promised myself to say yes to all invitations, I agreed to have a coffee while she dined.

She picked me up and we went to an Italian restaurant that was located near the mall. The restaurant wasn't very crowded, and I immediately realized that one of the waiters was an ex-boyfriend of mine, Phil.

Phil and I had met at an actors en masse ten years earlier. The evening we met, the director cast us together as husband and wife. We were both single parents at the time and were totally fascinated with one another. We dated for a couple of months before drifting apart. However, we remained friends and were always happy to run into one another at auditions. Phil had gotten married a few years after our breakup and had another son.

Lauren and I asked to sit in his section. Lauren ordered her lunch and I had my coffee. I asked him how the wife and kids were. He responded that the kids were fine, but he was getting divorced. I replied with, "Oh I'm sorry." He said, "I see that you got married." "Nope", I countered. I explained that the ring I was wearing on my ring finger was a souvenir from Italy.

We continued to catch up while Lauren ate her lunch. When he walked away to take care of another table, I asked Lauren if she thought it would be okay for me to ask him out for coffee. I never ask men out. She replied with, "Of course!" Lauren was very much a free spirit and would never think twice about asking men out. She used to live in a really cool warehouse space that had great wooden floors. She would sometimes ask men out with this great line, "I have an extra pair of roller skates. Do you want to come back to my house to skate around?"

When he returned to our table, I asked him if he would want to grab a coffee sometime. He said sure and we exchanged numbers. Then Lauren said that she was leaving and asked Phil to bring me home. I was shocked at her statement! Phil responded that he would be happy to.

When we got to my home, he came in to say hi to my mom. I thought that this gesture was very thoughtful.

He called me a few days later for a lunch date. We had lunch at Little Tokyo where we enjoyed sushi and riveting conversation. We were so happy! We felt so comfortable with one another and we laughed a lot.

He called me the next day to ask me out for dinner. We went to dinner that weekend at a funky Mexican restaurant in Mid City. I recall being a little nervous, yet excited on our first evening date in ten years. Would we have plenty to talk about? Common interests? Would he find me funny and charming? Would it go as well as our lunch date? It did! We had a really fun night. When we got back to his home, the first thing that he did, was call his sons, Sky and Dylan and check on them. He had them one week on and one week off. That evening when he kissed me good night, there was a spark and I knew that this was the beginning of something big. When I gazed into his clear, blue eyes, I knew that we would be together for an adventure of a lifetime! Within that first kiss lied the promise of forever.

A few years after dating, we had an intimate, but beautiful wedding at the Rose Garden in City Park, where we celebrated our love for one another with family and friends. Phil has been a wonderful dad to Madee and the boys and I get along amazingly well! Phil and I joke that even though our kids are now grown, they still want to hang out with us. There have been countless family vacations, holiday celebrations, and lovely family dinners where either Dylan, Madee, or I cook. The meal is usually followed by games or a movie. We have been together for over sixteen years and share a love for traveling. We love exploring London, Paris, and Ireland. We are especially fond of New York at Christmas when there is a possibility for snow, which is a rarity in New Orleans. On one particular visit, we sang "Baby It's Cold Outside" as we traipsed through Central Park.

Not every moment has been roses, rainbows, and unicorns; there have been several late nights of talking through issues. However, we work through the mis-understandings with love and respect for one another.

I share this story because it is amazing how drastically my life changed in one day just because I gave myself permission to say yes. It is as if the universe conspired just to bring us together for a fresh start.

Dare I ask the question? In what way do you think your life would change if you were not afraid of the consequences for saying yes? Maybe doors would open for a new job, a new love interest, new friendships, and new adventures. Have an open heart and an open mind. Say yes!

The Perfect Day Scripture

But the path of the just is like the shining sun, that shines
ever brighter unto the perfect day.

Proverbs 4:18

Prayer Notes

Printed in the United States
by Baker & Taylor Publisher Services